AmericanGirl Library®

The Quiz Book 2

By
Sarah Jane Brian

Illustrated by
Debbie Tilley

American Girl®

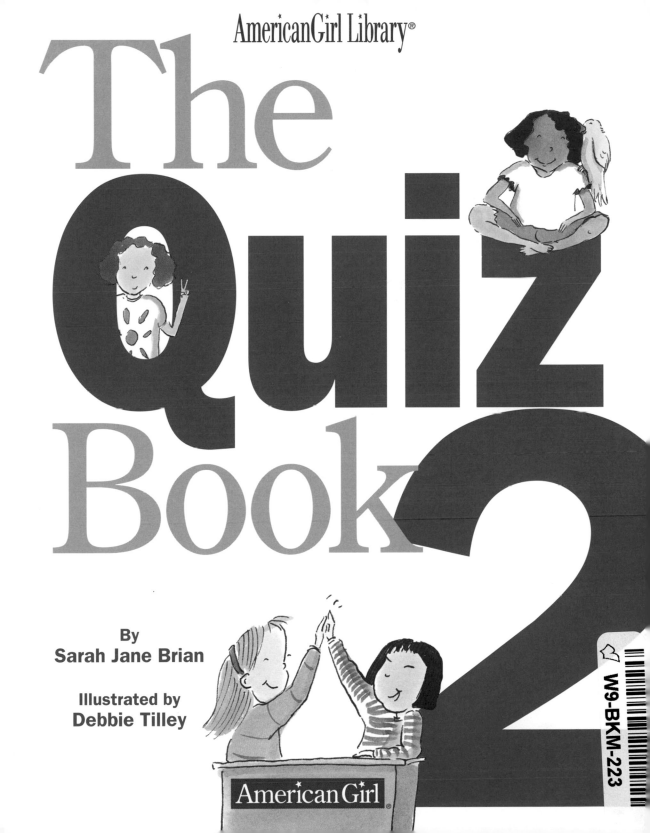

Dear Reader,

Do you love **discovering secrets?**
❏ **yes** ❏ **no**

Do you like to **laugh?**
❏ **yes** ❏ **no**

Do you have a **pencil** and a **comfy chair?**
❏ **yes** ❏ **no**

If you answered yes to all these questions, you're ready for

The Quiz Book 2! What better way to reveal your **true feelings**

and talents than through a quiz? You'll find out if you make a good

first impression, what your **dream career** is, if you're **ready to**

babysit, and much more! Be sure to **share the quizzes** with family

and friends to **discover their secrets,** too.

Now **plop down** in that comfy chair, grab a pencil and a pal,

and **enjoy!**

Your friends at American Girl

Contents

Pup Quiz **5**

How Embarrassing! **9**

Perfect Pals **12**

Party Girl **14**

The Secret's Out of the Bag! **17**

Sister Act **19**

22 Leader or Follower?

24 Does Your Confidence Shine?

27 Show Me the Money

30 Pet Check

33 Study Style

37 First Impressions

Doodle Dictionary **41**

Are You Superstitious? **44**

Myth or Fact? **47**

How Do You Compete? **50**

The Nose Knows **53**

54 The Amazing Sister Predictor!

57 Are You Thoughtful?

60 Help Wanted

64 The Right Words

67 Are You Ready to Babysit?

What's Your Sports Style? **70**

Can You Talk to the Animals? **72**

Snack Secrets **76**

Head in the Clouds **78**

Pup Quiz

If you had a wet nose and a furry tail, just what kind of dog would you be? To find your **pooch personality,** choose the answer that describes you best.

1. When it comes to sports, you have the most fun . . .

a. cheerleading.

b. snowboarding.

c. running.

d. doing gymnastics.

e. swimming.

f. being part of a team.

2. Your dream career is to be . . .

a. a fashion designer.

b. a top executive for a toy company.

c. an author.

d. a movie actor or comedian.

e. a pediatrician.

f. a professional athlete.

3. During the next school election, you'll . . .

a. lead campaign cheers for your favorite candidate.

b. run for president!

c. vote for your favorite candidates but stay out of the limelight.

d. write funny slogans and speeches as a campaign manager.

e. organize friendly debates between candidates.

f. have a hard time deciding whom to vote for, since you're friends with all the candidates.

4. Your dream vacation is . . .

TRAVEL AGENCY

a. celebrity-spotting in Hollywood.

b. exploring caves deep underground.

c. staying with your family in a cabin out in the middle of nowhere.

d. going to circus camp.

e. skiing in the mountains with your best friend.

f. living with a family in a different country for a few months.

5. The *Wizard of Oz* character you are most like is . . .

a. the glamorous Good Witch.

b. Dorothy, the leader of the group.

c. the Wizard, who likes to stay out of sight.

d. the funny and fast-thinking Scarecrow.

e. the sweet and tender Tin Man.

f. the friendly and some-times silly Lion.

6. Your favorite thing to do with a friend is . . .

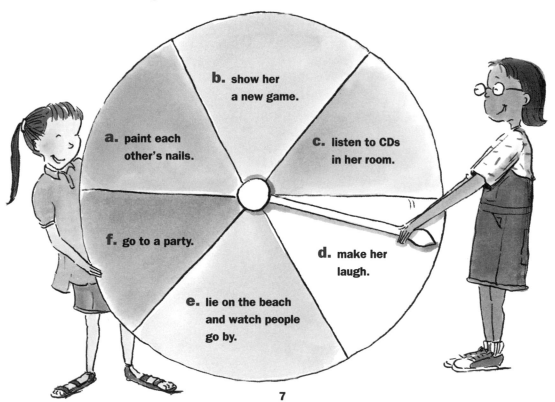

b. show her a new game.

a. paint each other's nails.

c. listen to CDs in her room.

f. go to a party.

d. make her laugh.

e. lie on the beach and watch people go by.

Answers

Mostly **a**'s

A **poodle** is the pooch you take after. Like this show dog, you are elegant and energetic. You also may be choosy at times—you know what you like, and you won't settle for less!

Mostly **b**'s

An **Airedale terrier** is bold and adventurous—and so are you! Like the Airedale, you also probably like to be the top dog.

Mostly **c**'s

You are most like a **greyhound.** Shy with strangers, you are devoted to your close friends and family.

Mostly **d**'s

Your pooch personality is a **cocker spaniel.** Playful and confident, you're a born comedian. You have lots of talents, and you probably love to show them off!

Mostly **e**'s

A **Saint Bernard** is the dog you're most like. You are easygoing, gentle, and calm. You are deeply loyal to friends and family.

Mostly **f**'s

You take after a **golden retriever.** Outgoing and warm, you are a friend to all you meet. You love learning, playing games and sports, and having fun, fun, fun!

How Embarrassing!

Your heart's racing, and your ears are turning **red.**
You're embarrassed! So, how do you handle it?
Choose the answer that best describes what you'd do.

1. When your teacher asks who knows the capital of Texas, your hand shoots up first. "Dallas!" you answer smugly. Wrong! You . . .

a. turn bright red and vow never to raise your hand again.

b. sink down in your chair and decide to study state capitals every night this week so you'll be better prepared next time.

c. say jokingly, "Well, I was just thinking they should move the capital to Dallas!"

2. While carrying your cafeteria tray, you trip and slosh tomato soup on your shirt. Everyone in line starts clapping! You . . .

a. call your dad to come take you home.

b. put on your jacket and zip it all the way up to hide the stain.

c. fall to the ground clutching the red spot and pretending you're mortally wounded.

3. You buy your friend a CD for her birthday. As she's unwrapping it, you remember you bought her the same one last year! Oops. You . . .

a. keep quiet and out of sight for the rest of the party, then go home early.

b. say, "I can't believe I forgot that you already have this CD! I'll take it back and exchange it for you."

c. say, "Isn't this great? Now you can play the CD on two boom boxes at once and get incredible stereo sound!"

4. After strolling out of the girls' room, you notice people pointing at you and giggling. Oh no! A long piece of toilet paper is stuck to your shoe. You . . .

a. run back into the bathroom and don't come out until the bell rings.

b. unstick the paper, shrug your shoulders, and walk on.

c. laugh out loud and point to your foot.

5. You're performing a dance with several girls in a talent show when you suddenly forget a step. You . . .

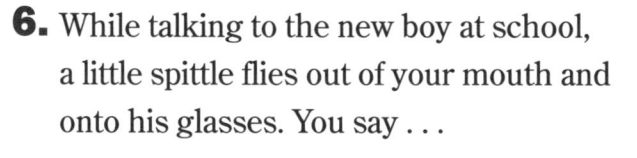

a. run offstage in the middle of the song.

b. stop for a second until you remember the next step.

c. start doing any crazy movement you can think of.

6. While talking to the new boy at school, a little spittle flies out of your mouth and onto his glasses. You say . . .

a. "Oh, never mind," and go away.

b. "Oops! I hate it when that happens," and keep talking anyway.

c. "Hey! Is it raining in here?"

7. You and your family are having dinner with the new neighbor when you knock over the gravy and it dribbles into the neighbor's lap. You . . .

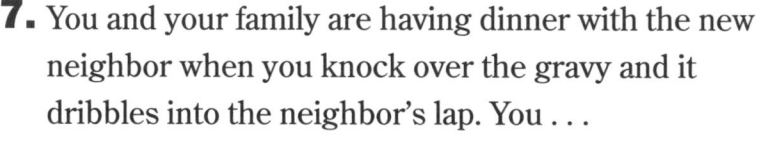

a. slink into the kitchen and pretend to start the dishes.

b. mutter, "Sorry," and mop up the spill with your napkin.

c. giggle and ask, "Would you like fries with that?"

8. You overslept, and you're really late for school. That means to get to your seat, you'll have to walk in front of the whole class. You decide to . . .

a. ask your mom if you can stay home today.

b. walk to your seat as fast as possible and get it over with.

c. interrupt the teacher and joke that you're late because you were kidnapped by aliens.

Answers

Mostly a's
Humiliation Hider

When you're embarrassed, your first instinct is to flee. But all that running may mean that you are worrying way too much. Most of the time, other **people won't even notice** what happened! Even if they do, **they'll forget it** long before you do. And sometimes, making a dramatic exit draws even more unwanted attention. The next time you feel the urge to escape, try letting a minute go by before you react. The embarrassment will ease, and everyone else will probably let it pass, too.

Mostly b's
Bounce-Back Champ

When embarrassing things happen, you try not to make a big deal out of them. Instead, **you deal with them the best you can** and get back to whatever you were doing. You still feel embarrassed, but because you don't show it much, people are less likely to tease you about it.

Mostly c's
Cool Comedian

You cope with uncomfortable situations by making a joke out of them. It's almost like saying, "I meant to do that!" This can be a terrific way to show that you don't take yourself—or the embarrassing situation—too seriously. **A good laugh** can break up the tension you may feel. Keep in mind, though, that there are serious occasions when being a comedian may not be your best bet. At those times, try simply smiling and moving on or, if appropriate, offer an apology.

Perfect Pals

Find out what kind of girls you tend to **befriend.** Follow the arrows to the answers that describe you best.

Start

What kind of band would you want to play in?

country →

hip-hop ↓

rock ↓

Do you like having lots of friends or one or two best friends?

one or two best friends ↓

lots of friends ↓

What's on your favorite T-shirt?

your favorite team's logo

a cute or funny picture ↓

How often do you call your best friend?

just when there's something important to say

at least twice a day, no matter what! ↓

You like having a friend who can . . .

be the life of the party

teach you new soccer tricks ↓

give good advice when you're sad

On a Saturday afternoon, you love to . . .

play Frisbee in the park

watch a funny video ↓

You think a great gift for your friend would be . . .

a poster of her favorite athlete

a diary ↓

You dream of doing this with a friend:

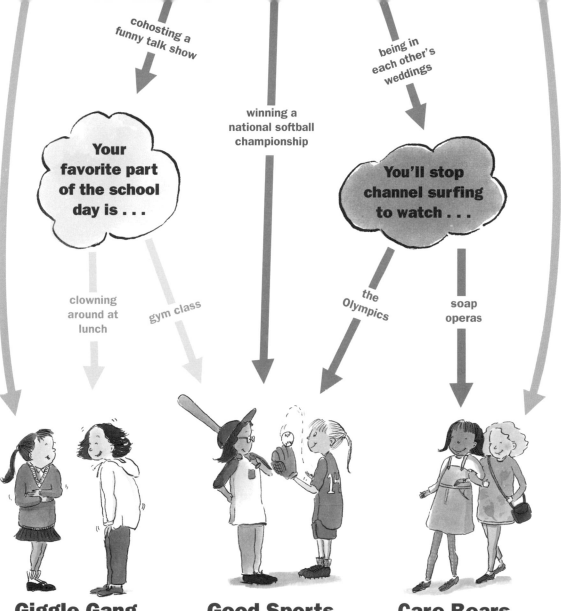

cohosting a funny talk show

being in each other's weddings

winning a national softball championship

Your favorite part of the school day is . . .

You'll stop channel surfing to watch . . .

clowning around at lunch

gym class

the Olympics

soap operas

Giggle Gang

You love to laugh! Whether you're in a big group or just hanging out with one pal, you're drawn to funny, outgoing girls.

Good Sports

You like your friends to be athletic and always ready to play. For you, making friends on a sports team is just as important as playing your best.

Care Bears

You treasure the friendship of girls who show they care. Knowing they're always there to support you and share close moments is important to you.

Friendship tip: Don't rule out a friendship just because a girl doesn't match a description from the quiz. If you have lots of interests, all different kinds of girls could be good friends for you. You never know what a new friend might have to offer!

Party Girl

Do you know what it takes to be a **great hostess?**

1. You've finished addressing the invitations to your birthday party, which your parents limited to ten guests. You . . .

a. hand the invitations out the next day in class.

b. wait until recess to hand them out.

c. mail the invitations or drop them off at your friends' houses.

2. A girl who's heard about the party comes up to you and asks why she hasn't received her invitation. You . . .

a. pretend it got lost in the mail, and then beg your parents to let you add a guest.

b. explain nicely that your parents limited the number of kids you could invite.

c. say, "What party? I'm not having a party."

3. It's 2:55 P.M. and your guests are arriving at 3:00. You are . . .

a. double-checking to make sure there are enough paper plates and napkins on the snack table.

b. just about to step into the shower.

c. racing around picking up your little sister's toys that are all over the living room.

4. *Dingdong!* Your first guest rings the doorbell. You . . .

a. yell, "It's open! Come on in!"

b. show her in, then go make a phone call.

c. open the door, hang up her jacket, and sit on the couch talking with her until the next guest arrives.

5. Emily and Anna have never liked each other much. But when they start arguing loudly at your party, you . . .

a. take them aside and quietly ask them to stop fighting.

b. ask them both to leave.

c. cry, "You're ruining my party!"

6. The pizza arrives! You . . .

a. make sure everyone else gets the slice she wants before taking your own.

b. yell, "Come and get it!" and join in the feeding frenzy.

c. push your way to the front to make sure you get a slice of pepperoni. After all, it's *your* birthday.

7. One of your gifts is a hideous green sweater. When you open it, you . . .

a. make a face and put the sweater aside.

b. laugh hysterically and say, "This is a joke, right?"

c. smile and thank your friend.

8. When the party's over, you . . .

a. admire your gifts while your friends wait for their parents.

b. walk everyone to the door and thank each friend for coming.

c. run off to play video games while your parents clean up.

Answers

1. c Since you can't invite everyone at school, it's best to give out your invitations more privately. That way, there's less chance of hurting an uninvited girl's feelings.

2. b Even if you give out invitations privately, someone you haven't invited may hear about your party and want to come. It's best to be honest but kind. Let the girl know the reason you can't invite her, but if you are interested in becoming closer friends, ask her to come over to your house another time.

3. a As the hostess, you should be ready to greet your guests when they arrive. It shows that having them at your party is important to you. Besides, if the guests have to sit around waiting for you, they're likely to get bored, and that's no way to start a party!

4. c Keep in mind that your guest probably isn't familiar with your home. It's up to you to make her feel comfortable and welcome.

5. a Asking your fighting pals to leave or yelling at them in front of everyone will just create more of an unpleasant scene. Instead, tell them calmly how much you value your friendships with them, and ask them to keep their bad feelings under wraps—for you.

6. a Oh sure, you've probably been to lots of parties where everyone just dives right in and getting your food is a free-for-all. But if you want to be a tip-top hostess, make sure that everyone else has what she needs first.

7. c You've heard it before—always say "thank you" for a gift. After all, what counts is that your friend thought of you on your birthday. And saying "thanks" doesn't mean you'll actually have to wear the sweater— just that you are grateful for your friend's good wishes.

8. b The gifts are open and the games have been played, but your job as hostess isn't finished until your friends are out the door and on their way home. Helping your parents clean up is a good idea, too— it shows you appreciate all the work they put into your party. Pitching in also makes it more likely that they'll let you have another party in the future!

The Secret's Out of the Bag!

What do the **contents of your backpack** say about you? Read the report and circle the answer in each box that describes you best.

Backpack Secrets Revealed!

by _____
Write your name here.

As the school year goes on, my backpack seems to
- get heavier and heavier
- stay about the same weight
- get left at home a lot
.

Of course, I'm not hauling around rocks in there, but I always feel like I need to carry
- all my schoolbooks, just in case
- only the books I'll need that day in class
- a few books, though I'm not sure which ones
. All my old homework and test papers from last semester are
- crumpled at the bottom of my pack
- stored in folders at home
- probably around somewhere . . .
.

When I have to take notes in class, I reach into my pack for a pencil, and I
- find so many I don't know which to choose
- find my favorite one right where I always keep it
- come up empty
. Then, I need something to write on, so I grab
- my chunky ten-subject, fur-covered spiral notebook
- the thin notebook I use just for this class
- the kid next to me and ask for a sheet of paper
.

Of course, every kid likes to make her backpack special in some way. To personalize mine, I
- display my entire key-chain collection on it
- keep one cute key chain dangling from the zipper
- planned to sew on patches, but I never got around to it
.

Answers

Now add up how many answers you circled of each color. If you circled mostly . . .

Pink

You like to carry everything with you so that you always know where it is. But let's face it—lugging around that heavy pack is no fun, and it's bad for your back. Plus it's **hard to find what you need** when your pack is so crowded. Hmm . . . do you think it's time to lighten up?

Purple

Your pared-down pack shows that you are **extremely organized.** Most of the time, you are prepared without being overloaded. Carry on!

Green

The contents of your backpack are a mystery to you, and **you often wind up unprepared.** Try making a list each night of what you'll need in school the next day. Then fill up your bag. You'll have a perfect pack in no time!

Sister Act

Are you a **good sib?** Pick the answer that describes you best. Be honest!

1. Both you and your sister always want to ride in the front seat of the car. So when it's time to go somewhere, you race as fast as you can and push her out of the way to get to the car door first.

   a. That's me.

   b. That sometimes happens.

   c. That never happens.

2. Your mom had to miss your dance recital last week, but now the whole family's going to your brother's concert. You're so upset, you sulk all the way there in the car and refuse to clap for your brother.

   a. That's me.

   b. I might do that.

   c. I'd never do that.

3. Your little sister is in your school this year. Whenever you see her in the halls, you pretend you don't know her.

   a. That's me.

   b. I might do that.

   c. I'd never do that.

4. The dinner dishes are clean, and everyone's done with homework. It's time for the usual: you get in a big fight with your siblings over what to watch on TV tonight.

    a. That's me.

    b. That happens once in a while.

    c. That never happens.

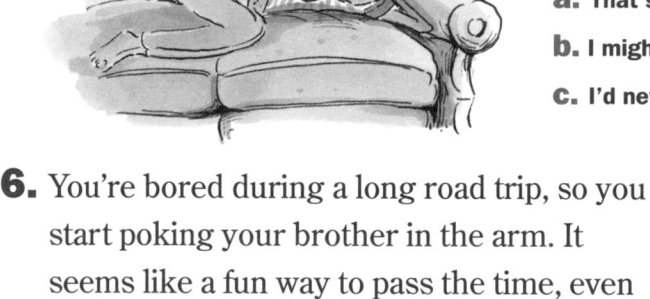

5. Your teenage sister is on the phone *again*. You run to your dad to complain and try to get her punished.

    a. That's me.

    b. I might do that.

    c. I'd never do that.

6. You're bored during a long road trip, so you start poking your brother in the arm. It seems like a fun way to pass the time, even when he yells, "Cut it out!"

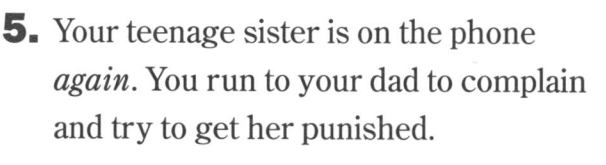

    a. That's me.

    b. I might do that.

    c. I'd never do that.

7. You are really proud of your spot on a gymnastics team. When your sister goes out for the same team, you're furious! You beg your parents to make her join a different sport.

    a. That's me.

    b. I might do that.

    c. I'd never do that.

8. Aunt Janice just sent over a box of homemade cookies. You're sure your brother will try to nab more than his share, so as soon as the box is open, you stuff your mouth with as many macaroons as it can hold.

a. That's me.

b. I might do that.

c. I'd never do that.

Answers

Mostly **a**'s

Constant Combat

Most of the time, you and your siblings treat one another like enemies. It may be time to call a truce. Talk about "problem areas" that often set off fights, and come up with ways to keep the peace. For example, if you're always bickering about who gets to sit up front, you might want to keep track of whose turn it is to ride "shotgun." And when something makes you mad, cool off before you confront your sib. Stay calm as you explain how you're feeling. Then really listen to your sib's side of the story, and try to come up with a solution together.

Mostly **b**'s

Struggling Sibling

You know you should try to control yourself, but sometimes you lash out at your siblings in spite of your good intentions. The next time your sister or brother is getting on your nerves, take a few minutes to think about the situation. Will fighting or complaining to your parents really improve things? Try taking a break from your sibling instead—go to a friend's house, or just hang out in a different part of your house for a while. Sometimes you need to spend a little time apart before you can be nice to each other again.

Mostly **c**'s

Keeping the Peace

You are doing a great job of getting along with your siblings. Even when a situation doesn't seem completely fair, you trust your parents and siblings enough to know that it will probably all even out in the end. By supporting and understanding your brothers and sisters, you've probably discovered that they aren't only a part of your family— they can also be friends.

Leader or Follower?

Do you **make things happen** wherever you go or would you rather **go with the flow?** Hit the trail to find out.

Start

When you get together with a friend, **who usually invites** the other person over?

a. **you** (move ahead **1**)

b. **your friend** (move ahead **2**)

Who picked out the comforter, wallpaper, and curtains for your room?

a. **your parents** (move ahead **2**)

b. **you** (move ahead **3**)

When you're with a friend, who usually **comes up with ideas** for what to do?

a. **you** (move ahead **2**)

b. **your friend** (move ahead **1**)

Your partner for a school project is telling you what she thinks the project should be, and you can hardly get a word in edgewise. **You have a different idea,** but you're not sure it will work. You . . .

a. **wait for her to finish talking, then tell her your idea before you decide.** (move ahead **3**)

b. **go ahead with the other girl's project, since she's so sure of herself.** (move ahead **2**)

A girl you want to become friends with **invites you** to go ice-skating. You've tried it before and hated it! You . . .

a. **suggest that you go bowling instead.** (move ahead **3**)

b. **grin and bear it—you can suffer through skating for a new friend.** (move ahead **2**)

On a class trip to the aquarium, a group of your friends is heading off to see the dolphins. **You prefer** the jellyfish, so you . . .

a. go with your friends now and hope they'll want to see the jellyfish later. (move ahead **4**)

b. talk a few other friends into going to see the jellyfish first. (move ahead **5**)

Your friend constantly talks about her favorite music group. You **don't really like** the group's music, so you . . .

a. pretend you like it. (move ahead **3**)

b. give your friend a tape of your own favorite band. (move ahead **4**)

When you go hiking, **who grabs the trail map** to figure out which direction to go first?

a. a friend (move ahead **1**)

b. you (move ahead **4**)

You go back to school in September, and everyone seems to be **wearing a new brand** of sneakers. You . . .

a. beg your mom to buy you a pair. (move ahead **2**)

b. stick with the new sneakers you have—you love them! (move ahead **3**)

Trailblazer

You **love to be in charge!** It's great that you are so sure of yourself—after all, you have great ideas, so why keep them inside? Just try not to let your enthusiasm keep you from listening to other people's opinions once in a while, too.

Middle of the Road

You **know your own mind,** and you're usually not afraid to share it. But you also know that you can't always have your own way, so you let others take the reins at times.

Along for the Ride

You're an **easygoing** girl who tends to let others make most decisions. That makes you a fun person to be around, because you're usually up for anything. When you do have a different opinion, though, **don't be afraid to speak up** and reveal the unique side of yourself!

Does Your Confidence Shine?

Do you trust in yourself, or do **challenges** make you weak in the knees?

1. School starts tomorrow, and you just found out your new teacher is Ms. Grimm. She's known for being the toughest teacher in the whole school! You . . .

   a. aren't too worried about it. How tough can she be?

   b. grill your older sister—who had Ms. Grimm two years ago— to find out if it's going to be as bad as everyone says.

   c. plead with your parents to get you switched into another class.

2. At school the next day, Ms. Grimm asks for a volunteer to read out loud. You . . .

   a. volunteer without thinking twice.

   b. first scan the page to see if there are any words you don't know.

   c. don't volunteer because you are nervous about reading in front of the other kids.

3. In gym, you're playing forward in a soccer game. Your team needs one goal to win. A teammate passes you the ball, so you . . .

   a. go for it—you think you have a good shot at a goal.

   b. dribble the ball closer to the goal, then pass it to a teammate who is more likely to score.

   c. pass the ball immediately. This is too much pressure for you!

4. At lunch, your friends are talking about favorite restaurants. You *love, love, love* Sushi Chalet, but everyone else is ranting and raving about Spaghetti Barn. So you . . .

   a. declare, "Sushi Chalet is the best!"

   b. say, "I like spaghetti, but I also like sushi."

   c. mumble, "You're right. Spaghetti Barn is the best."

5. Your band teacher asks if you'd like to try a difficult solo in the fall concert. You say . . .

   a. "It's a challenge, but I think I'm up to it."

   b. "Sure, if you really think I'm good enough," and ask for extra help to learn the music.

   c. "Maybe next year." You like playing with the group, but a solo would be too nerve-racking—what if you messed up?

6. Your assignment in art class is to draw a bird. You . . .

   a. draw a big, colorful bird from your imagination.

   b. ask your teacher if it's O.K. to look at some bird photos to get some ideas.

   c. ask to go to the girls' room, and dilly-dally as long as you can in the hallways. Maybe class will be over by the time you return.

7. After school, you try out for the lead part in the school play. When you see how great the other kids are, you think . . .

   a. I've still got a chance. I'll give it all I've got.

   b. Well, I can always be an extra.

   c. What was I thinking? I'll never make it.

8. At the school dance that night, you feel most comfortable . . .

a. doing the hottest new dance and teaching it to your friends.

b. dancing the one or two simple steps that you usually do.

c. hanging out by the snack table.

Answers

Mostly a's
Bold and Bright

The word *can't* just isn't in your vocabulary. You're an independent girl who knows that the key to meeting any challenge is to face it head-on with confidence!

Mostly b's
Catching Some Rays

You're confident, but you're also a bit cautious. You like to be prepared before you jump into anything, and you're not afraid to ask for the help you need to succeed.

Mostly c's
In the Shade

It sounds as if you need a confidence boost! Try this: sit down and make a list of things you have done well in the past, like the time you hit a double in softball or baked delicious brownies for your family. The next time you're faced with a challenge, take a look at the list and tell yourself, "I can do it!"

Show Me the Money

Welcome to *Show Me the Money!*—American Girl's
new quiz sensation.
Answer each question below with a friend in mind.
Then read your answers to her to see if you were right.

What would your friend do for one million dollars?

1. Eat a dozen live worms.
_____ **She'd do that.** _____ **No way!**

2. Sell her pets.
_____ **She'd do that.** _____ **No way!**

3. Move to Greenland.
_____ **She'd do that.** _____ **No way!**

4. Swim in a shark tank.
_____ **She'd do that.** _____ **No way!**

5. Agree not to watch TV ever again.
_____ **She'd do that.** _____ **No way!**

6. Chase a tornado.
_____ **She'd do that.** _____ **No way!**

7. Let tarantulas crawl up her arms.

_____ **She'd do that.** _____ **No way!**

8. Come to school in her pajamas.

_____ **She'd do that.** _____ **No way!**

9. Agree not to talk for one year.

_____ **She'd do that.** _____ **No way!**

10. Have a camera crew film her 24 hours a day for a year and broadcast it on TV.

_____ **She'd do that.** _____ **No way!**

11. Shave off her hair.

_____ **She'd do that.** _____ **No way!**

12. Eat chocolate-covered crickets.

_____ **She'd do that.** _____ **No way!**

13. Sing the national anthem to her favorite pop music star in person.

_____ **She'd do that.** _____ **No way!**

14. Wear orange plaid pants every day for the next ten years.

_____ **She'd do that.** _____ **No way!**

15. Spend a month handcuffed to her sister or brother.

_____ **She'd do that.** _____ **No way!**

16. Go skydiving.

_____ **She'd do that.** _____ **No way!**

17. Wade up to her shoulders in a swimming pool full of snails.

_____ **She'd do that.** _____ **No way!**

18. Make friends with the person she dislikes most.

_____ **She'd do that.** _____ **No way!**

19. Give up pizza forever.

_____ **She'd do that.** _____ **No way!**

20. Live on a deserted island for one year.

_____ **She'd do that.** _____ **No way!**

Answers

0 to 6 correct:
What your friend is willing to do for cash is pretty much a mystery to you. Oh, well—money isn't everything!

7 to 14 correct:
You have a pretty good idea of what's important to your pal.

15 to 20 correct:
Wow! Have the two of you been competing on a game show lately?

Pet Check

Test your **pet care know-how!**

1. Can furry pets get sunburned?

   a. Yes, especially in the middle of the day.

   b. No. Fur protects pets from the sun.

2. Which type of pet is sometimes afraid of the dark?

   a. bird

   b. cat

   c. gerbil

   d. none of the above

3. Which of the following is good for cats?

   a. milk

   b. raw fish

   c. chicken bones

   d. none of the above

4. What should you do right after you take your dog for a walk on a snowy day?

   a. Brush the dog.

   b. Wipe off the dog's feet.

   c. Give the dog some hot chocolate.

5. How much food should you give a tank of fish each day?

   a. about a teaspoon

   b. as much as the fish can eat at one time

   c. more food than the fish can eat at once so that they can nibble leftovers throughout the day

6. Why shouldn't you line an iguana's cage with newspaper?

   a. The reptile may become fascinated with the comics page.

   b. Newspaper gets soggy too quickly.

   c. Ink fumes can hurt an iguana, and ink may rub off on its skin.

7. How many hamsters should you keep in one cage?

   a. one

   b. two

   c. three

8. Your prize parrot constantly picks at his feathers. He could be . . .

   a. bored.

   b. hungry.

   c. excited.

Answers

1. a If pets stay out in the sun for long periods of time, they can get sunburned in places where they don't have thick fur. Pets with short, white hair and pink skin are most at risk. So rub a little sunblock on your pet's ears and nose—and your own—before going out in the sun together.

2. a Some bird owners even use night-lights to keep their feathered friends feeling safe and secure!

3. d Cow's milk is difficult for cats to digest. Raw fish keeps cats from getting an important vitamin called B1. And bones can cause choking. To keep your kitty in top shape, stick to cat food!

4. b Chemicals and salt used to melt ice on sidewalks can irritate paws, so it's a good idea to wipe them clean and dry them. If your dog's fur is wet, use a towel to dry her off, too. Brushing is a good idea, but it's better to brush before you go out into the cold, since a well-groomed coat will keep the dog warmer. And never give a dog chocolate—it contains a chemical that is poisonous to pooches!

5. b Give your fish as much food as they can finish in about five minutes. The amount of food you need will depend on how many fish you have. If you feed them more than they can eat at one time, the extra food will pollute the water and can make the fish sick.

6. c Newspaper is bad news for iguanas! Better choices are paper towels, carpeting, and artificial grass.

7. a Hamsters like to be alone—if you put more than one in a cage together, you will likely have a big, furry fight on your hands!

8. a Unless he's ill, your bird's bored. Try giving him a new toy or teaching him a new trick. Showing him lots of love should smooth his ruffled feathers.

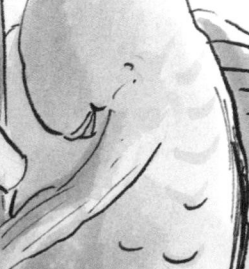

Study Style

Do you learn better by studying words or pictures?
This **memory quiz** can help clue you in to your own style of smarts.

YOU WILL NEED

A **timer**
or
a **clock** with a second
hand and a **friend**
to time you

1. Memorize the following list of words for **2 minutes.** Then turn the page.

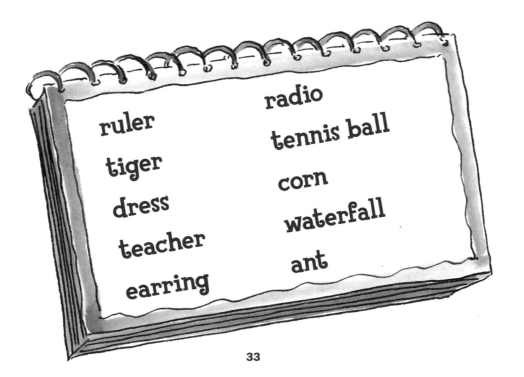

ruler

radio

tiger

tennis ball

dress

corn

teacher

waterfall

earring

ant

2. Take a break for **1 minute.** Walk around, do jumping jacks, or run in place.

3. When time is up, **write down as many words** from the list as you can remember in **2 minutes.**

4. Turn the page.

5. Now study the following pictures for **2 minutes.**

6. Turn the page and take another **1-minute** break. Make funny faces to pass the time!

7. When time is up, **write down the names of all the pictures** you can remember in **2 minutes.**

_____	_____
_____	_____
_____	_____
_____	_____
_____	_____

Answers

How many **words** from page 33 did you remember? _____
How many **pictures** from page 35 did you remember? _____

If you remembered **more words** than pictures, you are likely a verbal learner. That means reading and writing are great ways for you to learn. Rereading information over and over will help you when you are studying. Also try outlining the information you read.

If you remembered **more pictures** than words, you are probably a visual learner. That means things like pictures and photos help you learn and remember new information. When you are studying, try using a highlighter to help draw your eye to important points. Another tip: pay extra attention to charts, graphs, and maps in your textbooks.

First Impressions

Do you know how to **start out on the right foot?**

Answer the questions below to find out!

1. A new friend comes over to your house. You've never met her dad before, so when he comes to pick her up and rings the doorbell, you . . .

a. shout, "The door's open!"

b. open the door and invite your friend's dad in.

c. let your friend answer the door while you keep watching TV.

2. It's the first day of school. To make a good impression on your new teacher, you . . .

a. bring her a set of colored pencils as a gift.

b. wear a formal party dress.

c. volunteer to clean the blackboard.

3. You're going to a family reunion where there will be lots of cousins you've never met before. You . . .

a. bring your favorite board game to play with your cousins—that'll help break the ice.

b. bring a book to read so you won't have to talk to anyone before they talk to you.

c. bring a joy buzzer and some other practical jokes to play on your cousins.

4. Most of the people at your sister's engagement party will be from her boyfriend's family, and you're a little nervous about being among so many strangers. You tell your mom that you'd like to wear . . .

a. comfy old clothes to put you at ease.

b. a nice dress and your best shoes.

c. your older sister's clothes and makeup.

5. At the start of summer camp, you try to make new friends by . . .

a. asking other girls questions about themselves.

b. showing everyone the cool CD collection you brought with you.

c. handing out chocolate bars.

6. Your dad brings you to his office for a visit. When you meet his boss, you . . .

a. look around the room and don't say anything unless she asks you a question.

b. shake her hand firmly and say, "It's nice to meet you."

c. smile and stick close to your dad.

7. When you interview for a new babysitting job, you . . .

a. focus on showing the kids how fun you are.

b. let the parents ask all the questions.

c. ask the parents questions that you thought up beforehand and take notes.

Answers

1. b Your friend shouldn't have to answer the door—after all, it's not her house. Shouting "It's open!" doesn't let your friend's dad know that he is welcome. And watching TV instead of saying hello to a visitor is just plain rude.

2. c Offering to help out will get your teacher's attention and show that you are a considerate girl. A fancy party dress will make you stand out, but it isn't appropriate for school. Giving your teacher a gift may seem like a nice gesture, but it's not really appropriate either, and not necessary.

3. a Playing a game is a great way to start conversations with kids you don't know, which can help you get off on the right foot. Since you don't know your cousins yet, playing practical jokes is likely to make you seem mean rather than fun. Holing up in a corner to read by yourself will make others think you don't want to be friends.

4. b A nice dress lets people know that you want to help celebrate the occasion and that you're happy to be there. You may feel comfortable in old jeans, but the message they send is, "This event isn't very important to me." Wearing clothes and makeup that are too old for you isn't a good idea either. Instead, make an honest impression by giving people a chance to meet the real you—in your own clothes!

5. a Taking an interest in new people you meet shows that you are a caring person and a good listener who would make a great friend. Showing off a prized possession may get people's attention, but you want them to be interested in you, not your stuff. And handing out treats sends the message that you think you have to bribe people to get friends. Once the candy is all gone, the friends may disappear, too.

6. b This greeting is simple but effective, especially when meeting an adult. Look the person in the eye as you shake hands—he or she is sure to be impressed with your respectful manners and self-confidence. On the other hand, hiding behind a parent or avoiding eye contact reveals that you are nervous and uncomfortable.

7. c Let potential employers know that you're eager to do a good job. Ask questions like, "When is bedtime?" and "What are your rules on watching TV?" This lets parents know that you're responsible and you'll respect their house rules. Getting to know the kids is important, too, but your main role will be that of caregiver, not playmate.

Doodle Dictionary

Daisies, dogs, or dots—take another look at the doodles you draw during class. Did you know that they may reveal **secrets** about you? Fill the box below with your **favorite doodles.** Then turn the page to find the **meaning** behind all those scribbles!

Draw your favorite doodles here.

Doodle Dictionary

Now look up your doodles in our dictionary and find out what they may say about you.

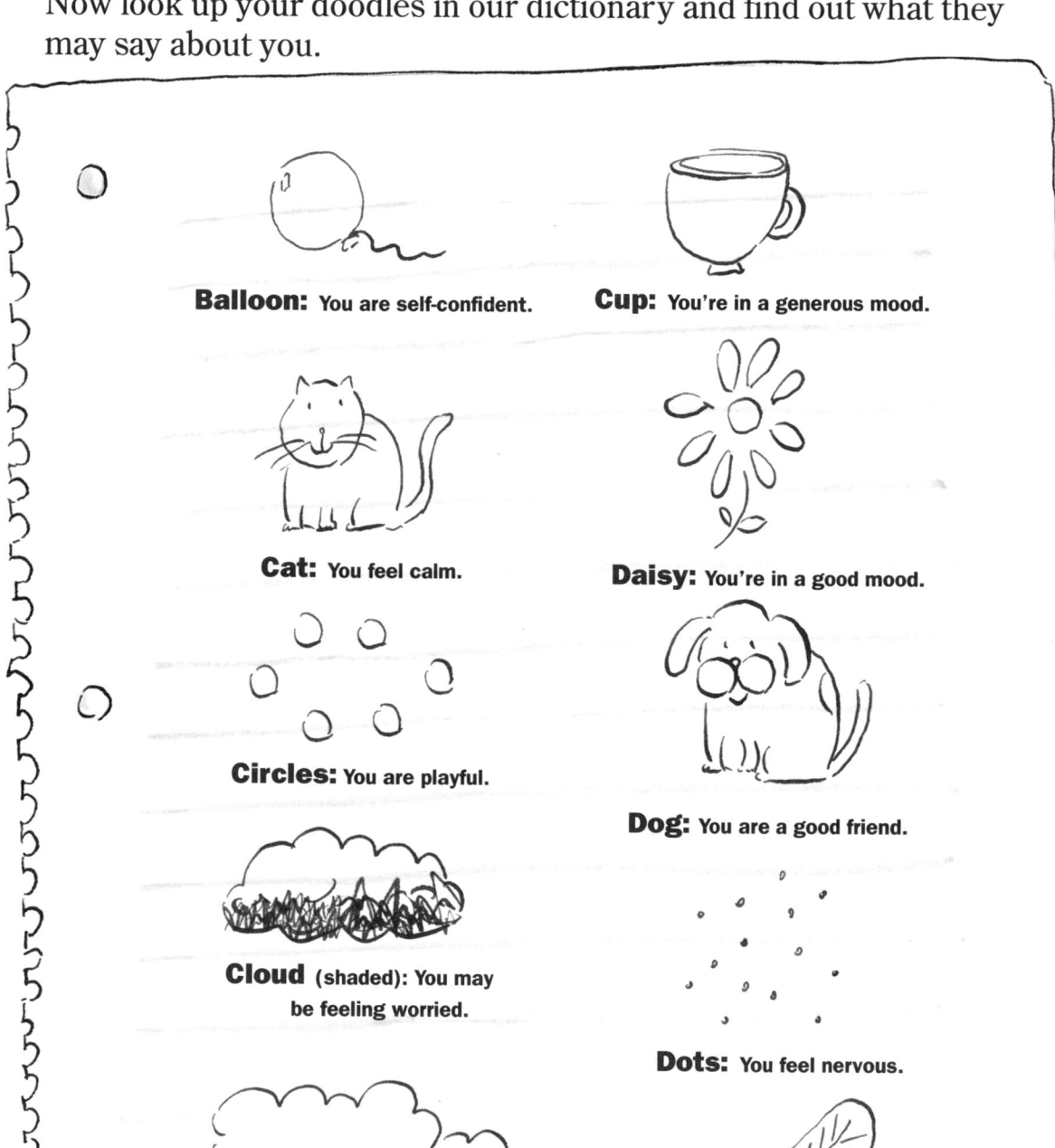

Balloon: You are self-confident.

Cup: You're in a generous mood.

Cat: You feel calm.

Daisy: You're in a good mood.

Circles: You are playful.

Dog: You are a good friend.

Cloud (shaded): You may be feeling worried.

Dots: You feel nervous.

Clouds (white): You are happy.

Feather: You want to be truthful.

Flowers: You love beautiful things.

Squiggles: You have a good imagination.

Heart: You're a loving person.

Stars: You feel hopeful.

Jagged lines: You feel angry about something.

Stripes: You're thinking about a problem.

Plus signs: You always look on the bright side.

Triangles: You have a lot of goals.

Squares: You like to follow rules.

Tree: If the branches are pointing up, you are reaching for new heights!

Are You Superstitious?

How much do you believe in **luck, wishes,** and other **supernatural stuff?** The answer is in the cards.

Start

CARD 1

You're on your way to a friend's house when a black cat crosses the street in front of you. You . . .

a. turn around and go another way to your friend's house. go to **Card 2**

b. keep walking but wonder if you'll have bad luck later. go to **Card 3**

c. reach down to pet the friendly kitty. go to **Card 4**

CARD 2

At a sleepover, some friends take out a Ouija board. You think . . .

a. it seems spooky, but you'll ask a few questions and wait to see if the answers are true. go to **Card 6**

b. it's great! You've been dying to know if you're going to get the part you want in the school play. go to **Card 5**

c. it'll be fun to ask questions, but you're sure it's your friends, not the board, who are pointing out answers. go to **Card 3**

CARD 3

You've worn the same socks to your softball team's last three games, and the team's won each time! You decide . . .

a. it's just a coincidence. go to **Card 4**

b. the socks must be lucky. You'll have to wear them to every game! go to **Card 5**

c. you'll wear the socks again if they're clean, but you won't go out of your way to do it. go to **Card 6**

CARD 4

At a carnival, you and a friend visit a fortune-teller. When the woman tells you that you'll soon go on a long trip, you . . .

a. giggle, since you know the farthest you're going is to Grandma's for dinner next week. go to **Card 7**

b. start packing! go to **Card 5**

c. ask your mom if she's planning a family vacation. go to **Card 6**

CARD 5

When you break a wishbone after dinner and get the larger piece, you wish for an A on your big social studies test. When you get the A, you think . . .

a. "Thank you, wishbone!" go to **Card 9**

b. "I wonder if the wishbone had something to do with my A?" go to **Card 8**

c. "Studying got me that A, not a dried-out chicken bone!" go to **Card 6**

CARD 6

Tonight is your first school dance, and you couldn't be more excited. Then you notice the calendar. It's Friday the 13th! You . . .

a. cross your fingers and hope the night goes well. go to **Card 8**

b. don't worry about it. You still can't wait! go to **Card 7**

c. stay home. go to **Card 9**

CARD 7

You're checking out the back of your new hairdo with a hand mirror. Suddenly, the mirror slips out of your hand and shatters on the floor. You . . .

a. wail, "Oh, no! Seven years of bad luck!" go to **Card 8**

b. help sweep up the mess—this isn't any different from breaking anything else. go to **Card 12**

CARD 8

When you go outside at night, you make a wish on the first star you see . . .

a. once in a while. go to **Card 11**

b. every time or almost every time. go to **Card 9**

CARD 9

You take a deep breath and blow out every single candle on your birthday cake. You're…

a. positive that your wish will come true. go to **Card 10**

b. not sure, but you're hopeful that the candles will help you get what you want. go to **Card 11**

CARD 10 She's a Believer

There's no question in your mind—you believe most superstitions really are true! But if superstitions are starting to rule your life, it's time to change your own luck. Try ignoring a superstition on purpose to see what happens. Go ahead and step on a crack, or just don't follow the advice in your horoscope. Then if you are still worried about superstitions, talk to a parent or another adult.

CARD 11 Wonder Girl

You can't decide for sure whether superstitions are true or false. Was it just a coincidence that a black cat crossed your path right before you missed the school bus? You don't think about superstitions too often, but you probably make wishes and have a few special things you do for good luck.

CARD 12 Keeping It Real

You find most superstitions pretty silly. Maybe you make a wish now and then for fun, but in your heart you don't believe that magic will make it come true. You know that the future is in your *own* hands.

Myth or Fact?

Some of these **old sayings** are absolutely true. Some are misguided myths. Take this health quiz to find out if you know what's good for you!

1. If you have allergies as a kid, you'll probably outgrow them.

☐ **True**
☐ **False**

2. Cutting your hair will make it grow in thicker.

☐ **True**
☐ **False**

3. Fish is brain food.

☐ **True**
☐ **False**

4. If you swallow gum, it will stay in your stomach for seven years.

☐ **True**
☐ **False**

5. Carrots are good for your eyes.

❑ **True**
❑ **False**

6. You should never wake up a sleepwalker because you might hurt her.

❑ **True**
❑ **False**

7. Eating chicken soup can help you feel better if you have a cold.

❑ **True**
❑ **False**

8. If you crack your knuckles, you'll get arthritis.

❑ **True**
❑ **False**

9. Looking at a solar eclipse can make you go blind.

❑ **True**
❑ **False**

10. Touching a toad will give you warts.

❑ **True**
❑ **False**

Answers

1. **False.** Sorry! Most allergies are never outgrown. Sometimes an allergy improves over time, but it's much more likely to stick with you even when you're an adult.

2. **False.** The number of hairs on a human head varies from person to person, but cutting your hair won't make new hairs appear. Still, don't despair—a haircut may make your mane look thicker by evening out broken hairs and getting rid of split ends.

3. **True.** Fish contains zinc, a mineral that can improve your memory. Fish is also rich in iodine, which helps your brain function well.

4. **False.** Chewing gum will move through your body just like anything else you eat. But you still shouldn't swallow gum—it can give you a bad stomachache.

5. **True.** Your eyes need vitamin A to help them adjust to different amounts of light, and carrots are a good source of vitamin A. So eating carrots will help keep your eyes healthy. But all the carrots in the world can't fix a vision problem you already have.

6. **False.** A sleepwalker is much more likely to get hurt by bumping into something while she's wandering around. But waking her might make her a bit confused. The best thing to do is gently lead the sleepwalker back to bed without trying to wake her up.

7. **True.** Unfortunately, nothing will cure a cold. However, scientists have discovered that chicken soup contains a chemical that thins out the mucus that makes you so miserable when you have a bug. So the next time you're feeling under the weather, grab a spoon and start slurping!

8. **False.** That's not your bone cracking—it's a bubble popping in the fluid found in your joints. The fluid is thick, like honey, which is why the sound is so loud. Cracking knuckles may be annoying for other people to listen to, but there's no evidence that it'll cause arhtritis.

9. **True.** Never, never look directly at the sun. Especially during an eclipse, the strong rays can cause temporary or permanent damage to your eyesight and even blindness.

10. **False.** This myth probably started because of the bumpy skin you'll find on some toads. But we're hoppy—er, *happy*—to report that it's absolutely untrue!

How Do You Compete?

Check off each statement below that sounds like **something you'd do.**

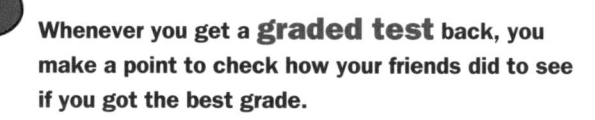 Whenever you get a **graded test** back, you make a point to check how your friends did to see if you got the best grade.

You think it would be fun to be on a **sports team,** but you've never joined one because you're not sure you'll make it in the tryouts.

You lose a **game of miniature golf** because you have trouble putting the ball. Afterward, you ask your mom to take you back to the course by yourself so that you can practice putting until you improve.

Another girl is on the **balance beam** at a gymnastics competition. You know that she is better than you, so you go into a fake coughing fit, hoping the noise will distract her.

Sometimes you set goals to try to beat your own best, such as making five layups in a row or reading ten more **pages of a book** at night.

Forget the sweat and dirt—your favorite spot at a sports event is **in the stands,** cheering on a pal.

 It's your sister's birthday. As she's **opening her gifts,** your brain is working overtime to figure out if her presents are better than the ones you got for your birthday last month.

 When you're out for a **bike ride with friends** and someone says, "Let's race to the top of the hill!" you hang back and watch the rest of them go.

 It doesn't matter if you **finish a test first or last.** What matters most to you is that you've taken the time to understand every question clearly and check over your answers.

 When one of your friends gets a **cool new pair of jeans,** you beg your mom for a pair, too.

 A friend asks if you'd like to **play on her Ultimate Frisbee team.** You've never played before, but the game sounds fun, so you give it a try and play your best.

 You're playing Scrabble with a friend who is really smart. So **when you win,** you do a victory dance around the board.

 You'd rather **play a video game** by yourself than play against someone else.

 When **playing Ping-Pong** with a friend, you think it's more fun to hit the ball without keeping score than to play a real game.

 You're **playing cards** with your sister when her hand tilts over to the side. If you leaned back a little, you'd be able to see what cards she is holding, but you resist the temptation to look.

Answers

Mostly

Obsessed with Success

It's great that you try so hard when you play a game. But if winning in all areas of your life is your only goal, you may be losing out. Close friendships become difficult if you are too competitive with pals, and sports and games may lose some of their fun if you can never relax and enjoy them. And if you cheat to make sure that you are the winner, you'll lose the feeling of pride in your victory. When you compete, **try to treat competitors as you want to be treated.** Everyone will enjoy the game more, including you!

Mostly

Worthy Competitor

Win or lose, **you always try to be a good sport.** You like it when opponents play their best, because it gives you a chance to test and perfect your own skills. If you lose, you know that you tried your best, and if you win, you know that you earned the victory. Once the game's over, you don't hold any hard feelings, which means you are ready to meet the next challenge head-on.

Mostly

Staying on the Sidelines

You usually avoid situations in which you'll have to compete. It may be that you're worried about losing. Or perhaps **you'd rather have fun with others** instead of pitting yourself against them. That's understandable, but taking part in at least some competition is important. It can help you in lots of ways, from creating new friendships to improving your self-confidence. Just remember that it's only a game, and go for it!

The Nose Knows

Beautiful **fragrances** do more than just smell nice—experts say they can actually **change how you're feeling!** Can you guess what each scent below may do for you?

 1. Lemon

a. banishes boredom and makes you feel confident

 **2.** Vanilla

b. comforts you and makes you feel friendly

 3. Cinnamon

c. wakes you up and makes you alert

 4. Lavender

d. calms you and allows you to breathe easier

 5. Peppermint

e. helps you concentrate better

 6. Orange

f. soothes you when you are upset or angry

Answers: 1. e, 2. b, 3. f, 4. d, 5. c, 6. a

The Amazing Sister Predictor!

Are you the **oldest, youngest, middle,** or **only child?** Let me guess! Check off the statements <u>on this list</u> that describe you best.

☐ You are superconfident—you believe you can do whatever you put your mind to!

☐ You love trying new things, even if you're not sure you will succeed. If it doesn't work out, it's no big deal.

☐ You've always felt very comfortable around adults, including your teachers and your parents' friends.

☐ Friends often come to you to help them work things out when they have a fight.

☐ You like to help your parents around the house.

☐ You have friends in lots of different groups, not just one set that you hang out with all the time.

☐ Your parents trust you because you've always been very responsible.

☐ You try to make sure that your after-school activities (like sports and clubs) are different from the ones your siblings are involved in.

☐ You love meeting new people.

☐ You often do things to get noticed, such as acting like the class clown or wearing an unusual hairstyle.

☐ Whether at home or at school, you always follow the rules.

☐ You're your own girl—you like to do things by yourself.

☐ You often let friends or family take care of little details. You're not much of a planner.

☐ You are a perfectionist—everything has to be just right.

☐ You find it very easy to make new friends.

☐ You don't really feel comfortable lending clothes, CDs, and other stuff to friends.

☐ When you get together with friends, you're usually the one who decides what you will do.

☐ Easygoing and flexible, you like to let friends decide what activity you'll do together.

☐ When you hang out with friends, they usually come to your house.

☐ You're full of mischief and seem to get into trouble more than most kids do.

Now our Birth-Order Fortune-Teller
will contemplate your answers and
make her prediction.
(Ahem, turn the page.)

Answers

If you checked mostly . . .

Blue

You're probably the **oldest child.** You have a drive to succeed, and you often take care of your younger siblings. You also try to please your parents as much as possible, and you like to take charge.

Pink

You must be the **youngest child.** You've learned a lot from your older siblings, but you often focus on being different from them. That way you won't have to compete with what they did at your age. You love trying new things, and you're not afraid to fail.

Green

All signs point to you being a **middle child.** Your older sibs are role models, but you also help look out for younger kids in the family. You're great at getting along with anyone and working out problems.

Orange

Your personality sounds like an **only child,** mature beyond your years. You are similar to a girl who's firstborn. You strive to succeed at everything you do and to make your parents proud. You're a natural leader, but growing up without other kids around may make it hard for you to share sometimes.

What? I Was Wrong?!

Don't be surprised if your personality differs from the typical girl with your birth order. The truth is, although studies have shown that birth order does have an effect on your personality, there's much more to you than just your place in the family. You are a unique person, no matter when you were born!

Are You Thoughtful?

Do you **do the little things** that count? Take this quiz to find out.

1. Rise and shine! You know your mom is under some stress because she's going to a job interview this morning, so you . . .

a. make her breakfast.

b. say "Good luck!" as she's walking out the door.

c. remind her to pick you up after swimming class tonight.

2. While you are waiting for the school bus, it starts to rain. You open your umbrella. You see a friend walking toward you with no umbrella, so you . . .

a. run to meet her and walk back to the bus stop with both of you under the umbrella.

b. share your umbrella when she gets to the bus stop.

c. hope her jacket is waterproof.

3. Another friend is out sick today. You . . .

a. pick up extra copies of your homework assignments and bring them to her so she won't fall behind.

b. give her the scoop on homework when she calls you after school and asks for it.

c. borrow an eraser from her desk since she won't need it today.

4. When Dad picks you up after school, you notice an empty hamburger wrapper on the floor in the backseat. It's probably your brother Billy's. You . . .

   a. put the wrapper in the litterbag, which is hanging on the back of Dad's seat.

   b. say, "D-a-a-a-d, Billy threw trash on the floor back here."

   c. ignore it—after all, it's not your garbage.

5. Your dad drives you to the mall to get a birthday present for a friend's party this weekend. You . . .

   a. remember some sparkly barrettes she admired the other day and pick them up.

   b. buy her a CD by your favorite band—if you like it, she will too, right?

   c. can't think of anything, so you get a gift certificate.

6. The next stop is swimming class. When it's over, most of the kids leave their kickboard floats lying around outside the pool. You . . .

   a. start putting them away.

   b. help out if the teacher asks you to.

   c. duck into the locker room so you won't have to clean up.

7. When you look at your planner, you see that it is your dad's birthday tomorrow. You . . .

   a. write a poem to read to him at dinner the next day.

   b. plan to tease him for being so old.

   c. hope Mom gets Dad the same cake she did last year. You love cream-cheese icing!

8. Your sister is studying for a big test tomorrow. You . . .

- **a.** offer to quiz her on her vocabulary words.
- **b.** use your headphones while listening to CDs so you don't disturb her.
- **c.** knock on her bedroom door every half hour to deliver knock-knock jokes.

Answers

Mostly **a**'s
How Thoughtful!
You're a girl who always finds a way to make someone's day. Being around you is a pleasure for others—and they're likely to return the favors by doing nice things for you, too!

Mostly **b**'s
Thinking . . .
You're a thoughtful girl who likes to help others, but you don't always go out of your way or do it the right way. To give your thoughtfulness a boost, try doing more of the unexpected every now and then. Give your mom an after-work back rub, or make a care package for a friend who lives far away!

Mostly **c**'s
Think Harder
You're probably an independent girl who is good at taking care of herself. That's a great trait to have. But don't forget that other people in your life are important, too. Try to think of thoughtful things you can do for friends, family, or people you meet. You'll find that you feel just as good as the person you're helping!

Help Wanted

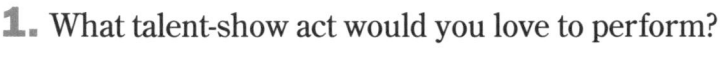

Tell us a little bit about yourself and your interests, and
we'll find **the perfect job for you!**

1. What talent-show act would you love to perform?

a. funny pet tricks

b. a dance routine with
a large group of friends

c. a skit that shows people
how they can help the
environment by recycling

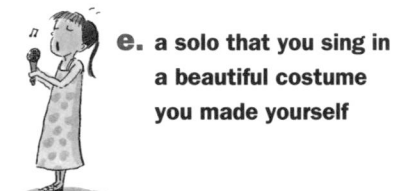

d. a magic act that
uses magnets,
mirrors, and puffs
of colored smoke to
amaze the audience

e. a solo that you sing in
a beautiful costume
you made yourself

2. When you're stuck in the car for a long drive through the country,
you like to . . .

a. count the horses, cows, and
other animals you pass.

b. have a family
sing-along.

c. daydream about how you
might make the world a
better place someday.

d. study the map and figure
out the best way to get
where you are going.

e. draw pictures or write
in your journal.

3. For a summer job, you think it would be fun to try . . .

a. dog walking.

b. babysitting.

c. volunteering to help build houses for the homeless.

d. setting up Web sites for your friends.

e. making friendship bracelets to sell.

4. When flipping channels on the TV, which show would you stop and watch?

a. a nature show about lions in Africa

b. a funny sitcom about friends getting along

c. a real-life story about people who rescued their neighbors from a flood

d. a science show that explains how the brain works

e. a craft program that gives great ideas for making your own stationery

5. Which homework assignment would you probably tackle first?

a. read a chapter of a book about dolphins and whales

b. make a family tree

c. write a history report about a hero you admire, like Rosa Parks

d. solve a page of math puzzles

e. write a made-up story that takes place on your favorite holiday

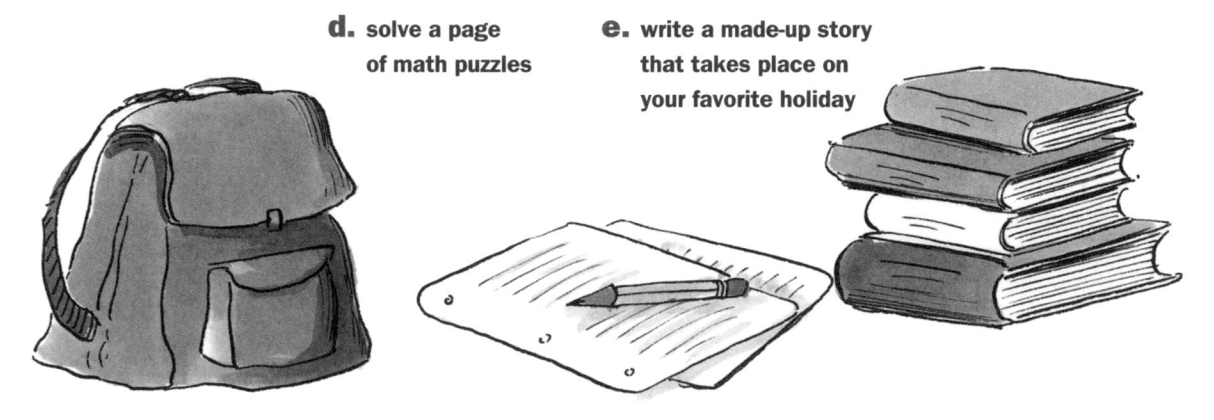

6. If you could redecorate your room any way you wanted to, what would you put in it?

a. a huge pet entertainment center full of toys and places for your pets to climb

b. extra beds to make sleepovers with your friends easy and fun

c. furniture and accessories made of recycled, environment-friendly materials

d. your own lab table for experiments, plus the latest computer equipment

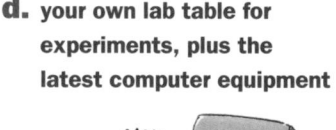

e. a big open space with special lights and a curtain where you could perform your own plays for friends and family

Answers

Mostly a's
Animal Magnet

You are crazy about creatures of any kind! You love to care for animals and learn about their ways. Your dream career might be marine biologist, veterinarian, zookeeper, animal trainer, or any other job that lets you work with animals.

Mostly b's
Personal Girl

Dealing with people gets your motor running. You are caring, friendly, and outgoing. You could shine in a career as a teacher, doctor, therapist—any job in which you spend lots of time with people.

Mostly c's
Dedicated Dreamer

You have high ideals—strong beliefs about how our world could be better—and you are full of hope for the future. Think about becoming a lawyer, politician, reporter, or fundraiser for good causes. With your spirit and dedication, you could make a big difference.

Mostly d's
Science Whiz

You're an intelligent, confident girl who gets a kick out of solving puzzles and finding out how things work. Scientist, architect, computer programmer, and engineer would all be terrific careers for you.

Mostly e's
Imaginative Creator

Creativity is your strength. You love to use your imagination and to express yourself. Your perfect career choice might be actress, writer, movie director, artist, fashion designer, or musician.

The Right Words

When you ask for something, how likely are you to **get what you want?** It might depend on the words you use.

What you want:

You'd like to sleep over at a friend's house tonight.
You think there's a good chance your mom will say "no way."

What you'd do:

How would **you** try to convince your mom? Circle the words below that sound like what you'd say, then find out what it means about your **power of persuasion.**

Answers

a. Not bad. **Offering a trade or a special promise** can often persuade someone to give you what you want. As the saying goes, "You scratch my back, and I'll scratch yours."

b. An **insult** like this won't get your mom on your side—it's much more likely to make her angry. And that means she'll probably turn down your request.

c. It's an **exaggeration** to say that "everybody" gets to do something. But even if it were true, this isn't a very convincing argument because those other people aren't involved here. The question is, why should your mom give *you* permission to sleep over?

d. These words might work. Maybe your mom can think of something that would make her decide in your favor, or perhaps she has a **compromise** in mind. On the other hand, she might be dead set against your idea from the start. In that case, you'll just have to accept the fact that sometimes, "no" is the final decision.

e. Hmmm . . . It seems pretty unrealistic that you'll never have to ask for anything ever again—which makes it unlikely that your mom will be persuaded to give you the permission you want. **Make sure you can deliver** on your promises!

f. Making a **threat** won't help your case. In fact, it gives your mom another reason to say no: she doesn't want to be blackmailed.

g. What's another name for endless begging and pleading? **Whining!** And as you probably know, most people (especially parents) don't like it. If your mom hasn't decided yet whether or not to give you permission, this tactic might just help her make up her mind—to say no.

h. Great thinking! You've used **facts and logic** to show why your mom should go along with your idea. Giving good reasons that your parents agree with can help you succeed in getting what you want.

66

Are You Ready to Babysit?

Take this quiz to find out if you have
what it takes to be a **super sitter.**

1. It's your first time babysitting at little Katie's
house. Before her parents leave, you . . .

> **a.** don't ask any questions—you don't want them to think
> you're inexperienced.
>
> **b.** go over your checklist one more time. Better safe
> than sorry!
>
> **c.** start playing with Katie right away. That's why you're there!

2. Freddie Jr. bursts into tears the minute his mom
puts on her coat. You . . .

> **a.** hand him back to his mom as she runs out the door.
>
> **b.** tell Freddie his mom will be back in a minute, even
> though you know it will be longer.
>
> **c.** distract him with a funny game.

3. You and three-year-old Amy are watching a
video together. "Potty!" she says. You . . .

> **a.** take her to the bathroom—now.
>
> **b.** ask her if she can wait. The movie's just getting
> to the good part!
>
> **c.** tell her to go ahead, and put the video on "pause"
> until she gets back.

4. *Boing! Boing!* Maggie won't stop jumping on the bed. When you ask her to get down, she says, "But my mom lets me!" You . . .

a. say, "Oh, O.K." and let her bounce.

b. say, "When your mom's gone, I'm in charge, and I want you to stop—now."

c. start jumping with her. She'll think you're the best sitter ever!

5. Ahhhh—the kids are finally asleep. You . . .

a. study or watch TV.

b. stretch out on the sofa for a snooze. You deserve a rest, too!

c. go through bookshelves and drawers to see what "interesting reading" you can find.

6. The parents have just returned, and you're ready to leave. Trouble is, they don't show any signs of paying you. You . . .

a. go home. They'll remember to pay you later.

b. remind them of your hourly rate.

c. stand at the door and patiently wait for them to catch on.

Answers
Give yourself one point for each answer you get right.

1. b Asking questions isn't a sign of inexperience—it shows you want to be prepared. The first time you babysit, arrive early and get the facts you need—like the number where the parents can be reached, when they expect to be home, what to feed the kids, their bedtimes, and emergency phone numbers.

2. c It's normal for little kids to cry when their parents leave. Luckily, it usually doesn't last long. Giving the child back to the mom will only prolong the tears. Instead, tell Freddie his mom loves him and that she'll be back by bedtime. Don't lie to him, though, if you know she'll be back much later. Then distract him with something new.

3. a When a toddler has to go, she means *now*. Since she's just learning, she'll probably need your help. Stop what you're doing and take her to the bathroom. Praise her for trying, even if she doesn't do everything just right. Help her wash her hands when she's done, and wash yours, too.

4. b Don't go along with any activity that you think is unsafe. Say, "Let's go outside and jump rope instead," or suggest a game to play. Later, tell the parents exactly what happened.

5. a You snooze, you lose! Once the kids are asleep, feel free to read, watch TV quietly, or do your homework. But don't sleep on the job—you might not hear the child crying or the phone ringing. Respect your clients' privacy, too. In other words, no snoopin'!

6. b Babysitting is your job, so don't be shy about asking to get paid. Say politely, "We agreed on $3 an hour, so that will be $9 for tonight. If you like, you can pay me tomorrow." Then call to remind your clients. Treat your job like a business, and they will, too!

How Did You Score?

0-2 points

Babysitting isn't for everyone, and it's O.K. if **it's not right for you yet.** Instead of kids, you might enjoy sitting for plants or pets—they need love and attention, too!

3-4 points

Your heart's in the right place, but **you might not be ready yet to sit solo.** Try being a mother's helper for a while. Watching the kids while Mom's at home is super sitter practice!

5-6 points

Congratulations! **You sound like a pro.** There's one important thing left to do: take a safety course. To find a class near you, ask an adult to call your local Red Cross chapter or visit www.safesitter.org.

What's Your Sports Style?

Are you born to perform, ready to go solo, or part of the team?
Take this quiz to find out **what type of sport** may fit you best.

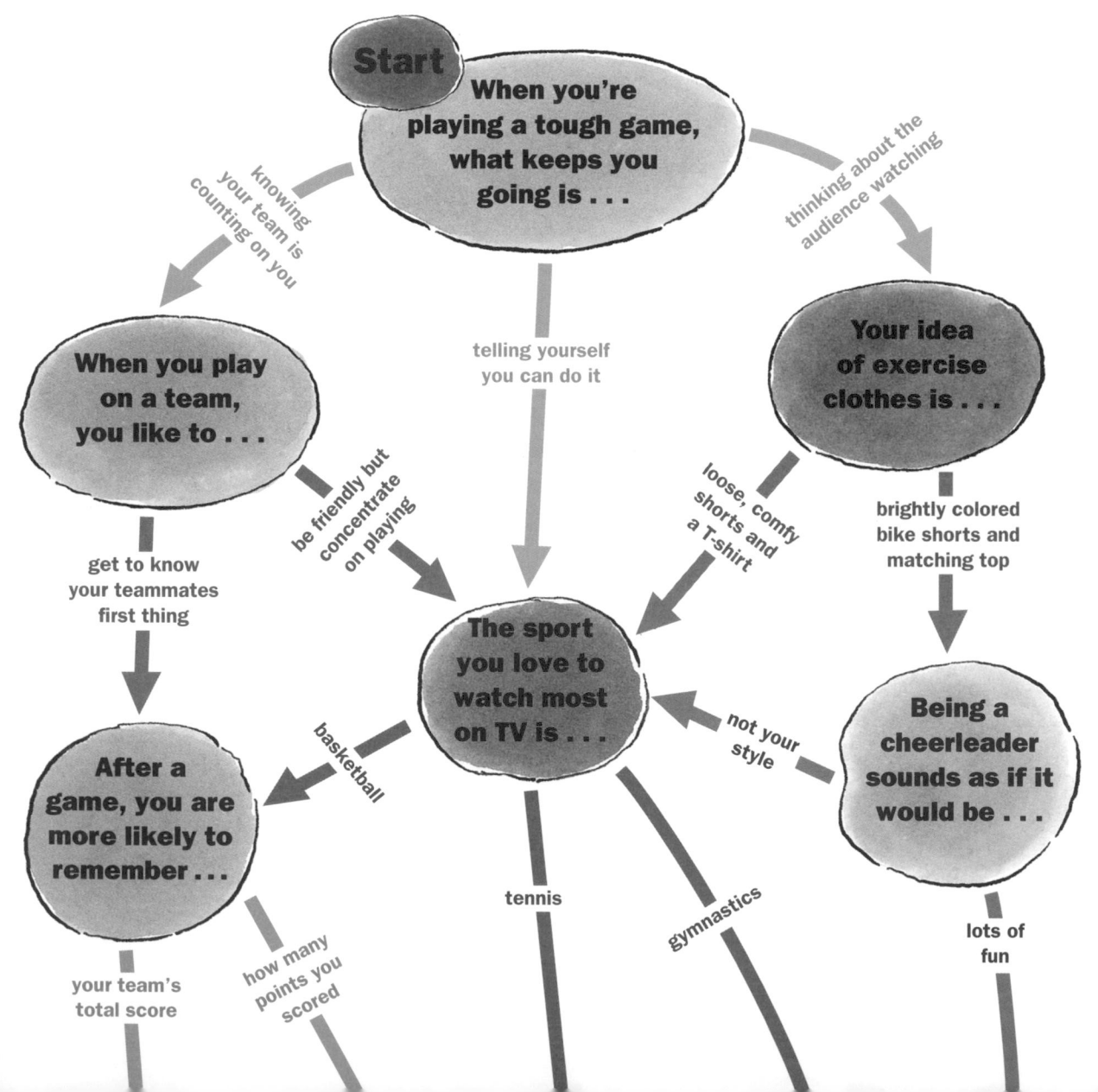

Start

When you're playing a tough game, what keeps you going is . . .

knowing your team is counting on you

telling yourself you can do it

thinking about the audience watching

When you play on a team, you like to . . .

Your idea of exercise clothes is . . .

be friendly but concentrate on playing

loose, comfy shorts and a T-shirt

brightly colored bike shorts and matching top

get to know your teammates first thing

The sport you love to watch most on TV is . . .

not your style

Being a cheerleader sounds as if it would be . . .

After a game, you are more likely to remember . . .

basketball

your team's total score

how many points you scored

tennis

gymnastics

lots of fun

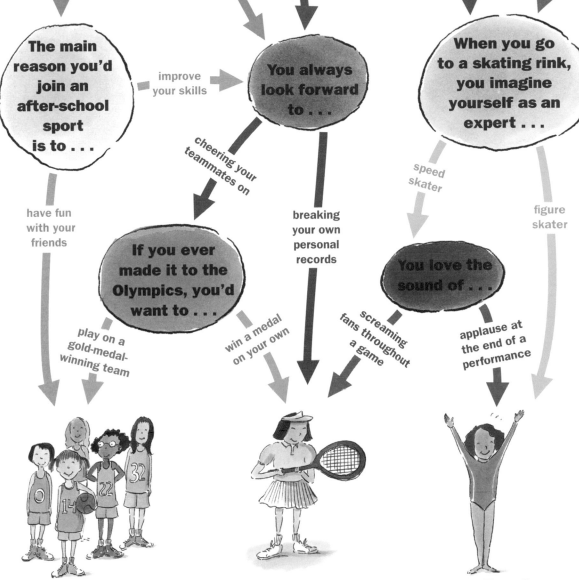

The main reason you'd join an after-school sport is to . . .

improve your skills →

You always look forward to . . .

When you go to a skating rink, you imagine yourself as an expert . . .

cheering your teammates on

have fun with your friends

breaking your own personal records

speed skater

figure skater

If you ever made it to the Olympics, you'd want to . . .

You love the sound of . . .

play on a gold-medal-winning team

win a medal on your own

screaming fans throughout a game

applause at the end of a performance

Go Team!

You get a boost when you play sports with other people, whether it's a formal team or just a bunch of friends. Team sports like volleyball, basketball, soccer, and softball are perfect for you. You'll also have fun doing group activities like biking, hiking, and Rollerblading.

Solo Act

No matter what sport you're playing, you focus on being the best you can be. You practice hard, and seeing your skills improve is a great reward for you. When it comes to competition, you may prefer to shine all on your own. Try a sport like tennis, swimming, running, or rock climbing.

Born to Perform

You enjoy sports that involve grace, beauty, and self-expression. Since performing in front of an audience gives you a thrill, try dancing as well as sports like gymnastics, figure skating, and synchronized swimming.

Can You Talk to the Animals?

Your pets may not use words, but they have a lot to say.
Do you know how to **read their body language?**
Take this quiz to see if you might be the next Dr. Dolittle.

1. Your dog leans forward with her front legs
on the ground and her rear end sticking
up in the air. She's trying to say . . .

a. "Scratch my ears, please."

b. "Let's play!"

c. "Can I have a biscuit?"

2. Your gerbil is thumping her two back
feet against the floor of her cage. Her
message is . . .

a. "Look out! There's danger nearby!"

b. "Feed me!"

c. "The floor of this cage is really dirty!"

3. While sitting on your lap, your cat squeezes his
eyes about halfway shut, as if he is squinting. This
clue tells you that your cat . . .

a. is trying to get a better look at a bird
that just landed outside the window.

b. is asleep.

c. is feeling very happy and relaxed.

4. Your classroom's pet rabbit lies down with all his feet hidden under his body. The bunny's head is stretched out and down in front of him. He wants you to . . .

a. pet him.

b. take him to the vet, since he's feeling sick.

c. trim his toenails.

5. To let your horse know you're not being threatening, you always approach her from . . .

a. the front.

b. the side.

c. the back.

6. When you walk up to your iguana's cage, his head starts bobbing up and down fast. This is his way of . . .

a. asking to be picked up.

b. getting some exercise.

c. warning, "This is my territory! Stay away!"

7. Two guinea pigs go up to each other and touch noses. They are . . .

a. cold.

b. about to fight.

c. saying hello.

8. Looking straight at an unfriendly barking dog is a bad idea because he may think it means . . .

a. you're too weak to defend yourself.

b. you're afraid of him.

c. you're challenging him.

9. You arrive home from school, and your cat walks over to you with her tail straight up in the air. She's saying . . .

a. "I'm so glad to see you!"

b. "Will you play with me?"

c. "I scratched up the couch while you were gone."

10. Your aunt's bird is sitting on his perch making clicking sounds. He's saying . . .

a. "I'm feeling friendly."

b. "I want to get out of my cage and fly."

c. "The hall clock just stopped."

11. Your horse's ears are pointing out to the sides and drooping down. That means she . . .

a. is angry.

b. feels tired and sad.

c. has an earache.

12. If your dog's tail is hanging down
between her hind legs, she is feeling . . .

   a. afraid.

   b. playful.

   c. relaxed.

Answers

1. b	**7.** c
2. a	**8.** c
3. c	**9.** a
4. a	**10.** a
5. b	**11.** b
6. c	**12.** a

Snack Secrets

Chew on this—a study recently found that your favorite **junk food** reveals secrets about you. We know it is hard to believe, but go ahead and **circle the snack** that you usually crave. Then turn the page to see if you agree.

Answers

Potato Chips
You are ambitious and successful.

Crackers
You are shy and thoughtful. You treasure time when you can be alone.

Pretzels
Full of energy and adventure, you love trying new things. Routines bore you.

Cheese Curls
You're honest and fair, with a strong sense of right and wrong. You usually plan ahead, and you keep your room neat as a pin.

Tortilla Chips
You care deeply about others, and you hate to see unfairness of any kind.

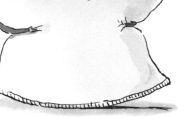

Beef Jerky
You're outgoing and generous. You're a loyal and true friend who can always be trusted.

Head in the Clouds

Look! **Up in the sky!** It's a bird, it's a plane,
it's . . . whatever you think it is!

Head outside on a day when lots of **fluffy clouds** are
floating by. Look at them closely. What shapes do you see?
A pineapple? A girl doing a cartwheel? A puppy?
In the blanks below, write down the first
five shapes you see.

Answers

If most of your shapes were **animals**, it's likely that you are a caring girl. You would make a terrific babysitter, and you are great at helping friends with their problems.

If most of the cloud shapes you saw were **people**, you are probably a very social girl. You like joining clubs, making friends, and spending time with groups of people.

If most of the shapes you saw were **objects**, you are probably quite independent. You like the feeling of accomplishment when you achieve something on your own, such as creating a painting or learning a new computer program.

Let us know what you'd do! Write to:

Quiz Book Editor
Pleasant Company Publications
8400 Fairway Place, P.O. Box 620998
Middleton, Wisconsin 53562

Or visit our Web site:

www.americangirl.com

Published by Pleasant Company Publications
Copyright © 2001 by Pleasant Company

Printed in China.

04 05 06 07 08 C&C 11 10

American Girl Library® and American Girl® are registered trademarks of Pleasant Company.

Editorial Development: Julie Williams, Michelle Watkins
Art Direction and Design: Chris Lorette David
Production: Kendra Pulvermacher and Janette Sowinski
Quiz Development: Gregory Smith, Ph.D.

Some quizzes in this book have previously appeared in *American Girl* magazine.